Founded on a rock

THE PHILOSOPHY OF SPINOZA
AFTER THREE CENTURIES

Dr. Albert Goodheir

GLASGOW
Kardo
1978

ISBN : 0 905149 06 8

Translated by the author from the original in Esperanto:
Fondita sur roko. La filozofio de Spinoza post tri jarcentoj.
(Kardo, 1977)

Illustrations by Ruth Goodheir

Published by KARDO, 16 Woodlands Drive, Coatbridge, ML5 1LE
Scotland

tel. 0236.21636 Giro 17 300 4008

Production by Fellowship Press, Gloucester

CONTENTS

ABBREVIATIONS OF SPINOZA'S BOOKS

Eth: Ethics, Lat.: Ethica ordine geometrico demonstrata.

ST : Short Treatise, Dutch: Korte verhandeling van God, de mensch en deszelfs welstand.

TRU : Treatise about the Rectification of the Understanding, Lat.: Tractatus de intellectus emendatione.

TTP. : Tractatus theologico-politicus.

TP. : Tractatus politicus.

INTRODUCTION

The house of our civilization is shaking; hidden cracks are now coming to light. We are discovering that we live in a house built on sand, and according to the biblical parable 'the rains descended, and the floods came, and the winds blew and beat upon that house, and it will fall, and great will be the fall of it.' Wars, ideologies that justify violence, and destruction of the environment have put an end to the illusive certainty of progress. But three centuries ago already, when the foundations were laid, one man knew that they were faulty and laid others, on which hardly anyone as yet has built. He was the Dutch philosopher Spinoza (1632 – 1677), whom the religious called an atheist and whom his own Jewish community excommunicated.

For more than a century after his death he was hated and his name became a byword. Orthodox Christians proclaimed that his books were forged in Hell with assistance of the Devil. But not only they, also 'freethinking' progressives misunderstood and feared him. References to him were rare, but seldom without venom. This fact is worth remembering, for it helps to breed a healthy suspicion of those that in any one period consider themselves progressive.

The great ones in the field of philosophy showed themselves small in their relation to Spinoza. Leibniz, who visited him in person, used his ideas but kept silent about his debt to him. Even Hume, the kind Scot in whose heart there was room for the intolerable Jean-Jacques Rousseau, spoke about the 'hideous hypothesis' for which Spinoza was 'universally detested'. Hegel, who based his philosophy on all that Spinoza distrusted, gave him a judas kiss of praise, but showed his true feeling by a bad German joke about Spinoza's death (a pun on *Schwindsucht*).

In the history of philosophy Spinoza usually gets a chapter somewhere between Descartes, whose system he knew and rejected, and Kant, who did not know him. But Spinoza is a critic rather than a part of the philosophic tradition of the West. History did not make him a philosopher of the philosophers. He is, and perhaps will be, the philosopher of the poets.

Lessing, Goethe, Wordsworth, Coleridge, Shelley, Heine, the Dutch poet Gorter and others loved him and learned from him. Shelley, shortly before his death, began an English translation of the 'Ethics'. Gorter made a Dutch translation.

In the nineteenth century interest in Spinoza arose also among philosophers and historians. There is no lack of books about him. I hope that I learned much from them; to mention some would be an injustice to others. In several bibliographies one can find books about Spinoza in many languages.*

I wrote this book not without misgivings. Like Spinoza, I have no wish to offend anyone. But I know that the ideas of Spinoza, if understood, are bound to raise hairs on the right and the left, on churchgoers and atheists, traditionalists and modernists. By his trust in intuition Spinoza frightens positivists, by his rationality he offends existentialists. But, as it happened to the prophet Jeremiah, the message of Spinoza became 'like a fire blazing in my heart, and I was weary with holding it under and could endure no more.'

Spinoza has been made to serve many ends. Many have tried to draft him into their ranks, as an atheist, a mystic, a Hegelian idealist, a Marxist materialist. Jews have hated him as a renegade, Christians and racialists as a Jew. In spite of them all, Spinoza remains Spinoza; traditionalist because he uses words, and language implies tradition; discoverer because he went straight to the heart of the All, which he loved and called God. He did what some contemporary philosophers consider impossible: he deliberately gave a new meaning to words, and so made possible an understanding which transcends words.

I wrote this book first in Esperanto, the International Language, because mankind, like the universe, is one and indivisible. Symbol of man's understanding of man, and the best vehicle of his thought, is a planned universal language, not a language that has spread only as the result of the power or

* Bibliographies:
Adolph S. Oko, The Spinoza Bibliography, Boston 1964.
Catalogus van de bibliotheek van de vereeniging 'Het Spinozahuis', Leiden 1965.
'Spinoza, Essays in Interpretation' includes bibliography by E. M. Curley (1960 - 1972). Open Court, La Salle, Illinois, U.S.A. 1975.

wealth of its speakers. Moreover, Esperanto, like Latin, helps clear thinking. Writing in English one is tempted to take to the air behind a smokescreen of jargon. My translation tries to keep its feet on the ground.

By the use of Esperanto I proclaim my conviction that those philosophies that lead to hatred between classes, nations and races are subjective and foolish, in spite of the fame of Hegel who prepared the ground for them. I do not expect that this truth will be widely accepted in a period in which violence is worshipped, and murderers are called freedom fighters. But this will pass, like all historical phenomena; more important is that which is timeless. Hatred, and the fear from which hatred arises, are unwise. Apart from ignorance nothing is really to be feared. The way to knowledge is the way to God which Spinoza showed.

So the die is cast. If I have done anything to counteract the cramp of the conservatives and the destructiveness of the revolutionaries, if someone discovers that opinion is not knowledge, if any reader has a new look at the universe and takes off ideological spectacles, I have not written in vain.

If the book deserves a dedication, I should like to dedicate it to those who love and protect Nature and the monuments of the past, to those who work for peace not by words but by personal actions, to the Religious Society of Friends (Quakers), whose members for three centuries have tried to worship God without putting an ideological screen before Him, and to those, all over the world, who joyfully and persistently keep alive the fact of the International Language and the hope of its worldwide acceptance as a second language.

Spinoza's house, Rijnsburg

CHAPTER 1. FOR WHAT PURPOSE?

In Rijnsburg, a quiet village between Amsterdam and The Hague, an old house stands far from the main roads. It bears on a stone in the wall a strophe of the seventeenth century religious poet Dirck Rafaelszoon Camphuysen:

> If only all mankind were wise
> and willing to do well,
> the earth would be a Paradise,
> now it is often Hell.

The builder of the house, member of the 'Collegiant' sect, friend and host of Spinoza, had those words engraved to witness to his conviction that not 'the world, the flesh and the devil' but human foolishness make a hell on earth. In that house Spinoza lived from 1661 to 1663; there he began to write his 'Ethics'. Visitors today, coming out of the silence of the two rooms where he lived and worked, hear the roar of distant traffic, which reminds them that they are in the most densely populated land of Europe. Why all this activity? Wherefore and whereto do people hurry? Can human actions, ultimately, have any rational aim? Must we not accept, as Hume did a century after Spinoza, that 'reason is, and must be, the slave of passion'?

Hume, who was one of the most reasonable of men and who lived in a period of stability, could afford to flirt with irrationality. Our generation has learned what it carries in its train, in man's mind and in his social life. Anyone today who does not ask 'What is the sense of living?' has already capitulated.

Those that seek an answer to that question will hardly get much help from contemporary philosophers. If they belong to the 'analytic' school, they will reply that the task of philosophers is not to guide others, but to talk to colleagues about the meaning of words. If they are 'existentialists', they will use all the reason they have to prove that reason is no good. If they believe in some kind of dialectic of Hegelian origin, they will quasi-objectively justify conflicts between groups, and the hostility without which immature and internally divided people cannot live.

Spinoza, like Socrates, was not a professional philosopher. He was a man who dedicated his life to the search for a worthwhile aim, and for the best way of attaining it. Listen to his own words, in the first chapter of his unfinished 'Treatise on the Rectification of the Understanding':

> 'After I had learnt by experience that all things that ordinarily fill our lives are vain and futile, when I saw that all worrying and frightening things were only good or bad according to their effect on my mind, I finally decided to find out whether there was anything really good, which could communicate its goodness to me and which could fill my mind to the exclusion of other things. In other words, I decided to find out whether I could find anything that could give me supreme and eternal joy.... That which seems to be people's ultimate aim can be brought under three headings: wealth (*divitiae*), rank (*honor*) and sensual pleasure (*libido*). They capture the mind, so that people can hardly think of anything else....
>
> (I concluded) 'that happiness or unhappiness depends on the nature of that which we love. That which is not loved does not cause conflicts. It causes no anguish when it disappears, nor envy when others have it, no fear, no hatred, in fact no emotions of any kind. These emotions are caused by the love for transitory things, such as the ones mentioned. Only the love for what is eternal and infinite fills the heart with joy and eliminates sorrow. This is a thing worth looking for, and the search of it deserves our complete dedication....
>
> 'Really good is everything that can help us to attain this goal, if possible together with other people. Later on I shall clarify this aim; it is to be formulated as the knowledge of the unity of the mind with all Nature.'

'The search for what is eternal and infinite.' Is the search for this really the inescapable condition of human happiness, the only possible basis of an adequate philosophy and a satisfactory style of life? Spinoza believed it and lived accordingly. If so, we have been barking up the wrong tree. By 'we' I mean the West for several centuries, and today the whole world, doing its utmost to imitate the West.

Those that keep alive the traditions of religion claim to seek the eternal, but usually not by rectification of the understanding, and by mutually exclusive ways. They have little influence on our conflicting social and economic systems, which agree in seeking the greatest possible production and consumption. Luxuries of one generation become necessities of the next. If the way of Spinoza were to become not a freak allowed to some eccentrics but an ideal of communal life, today's world would have to change into something very different.

Moreover, there remains the question whether this aim is attainable, and if it is, whether it is an ideal for a few only. Since Kant, philosophers have warned us that there can be no knowledge of the eternal.

Spinoza might well agree that there is not much hope for our civilization as long as its basic striving is after the transitory. To doubters he might reply that only those that seek the eternal with all their heart, might and strength are likely to discover whether it can be found. However, there is no doubt that Spinoza did not consider 'salvation', that means lasting joy, life without fear or destructiveness, as being for a few isolated individuals. One does not enjoy the highest good in isolation; who finds it wants to communicate it to others.

Spinoza did not have the illusion that all men could become philosophers. He believed, however, that religion cleansed of ideological divisions and a well organised society, in one word that which now we should call culture, could offer salvation to the majority of men. If this happens, it will not be because of any foreseeable historical evolution, or because of God's intervention; they both belong to the realms of illusions. It will happen only when men learn to use the capacities of their minds and bodies, and learn to distinguish between knowledge and imagination.

CHAPTER 2. GOD – ALL

Spinoza is reported to have said the philosophers of the scholastic tradition started from the senses, Descartes from the mind, but he from God. In fact, the knowledge of God is the basis of Spinoza's philosophy. In this he challenges not only his predecessors, but also those that came after him. Nobody followed him on this road. It is generally accepted that man can believe or disbelieve in God, but not know him. It is doubtful whether the proofs of God's existence ever convinced any unbeliever.

Modern people might well ask, whether the scholastics were not right in starting from the senses, and wrong only because they did not stop there. What contradicts science is rightly rejected, and science, at least by non-scientists, is taken to be a matter of sense data and conclusions based on them. It might be agreed that Descartes' method has failed. His dualism can relate matter to mind only by postulating an everlasting miracle. But there remains the question whether beginning from God one could arrive at anything apart from tautology.

It is to be noted that Spinoza did not start from any abstraction, any immaterial mind. From him physical experience is the basis of knowledge. From experience of phenomena he arrives, by rectification of the understanding, at knowledge of the whole.

If one thinks of the totality of all that exists as if it were a collection, one will never understand the thought of Spinoza. A cairn on a mountain top, to which every climber adds a stone, is not a helpful symbol of the universe. One can think of better ones. Chess, for instance, is not derived from the moves on the chessboard. The existence of chess by means of its rules makes meaningful moves possible. Another example: language is not a collection of words. The existence of language makes the meaningful use of words possible. Science is not a collection of facts. The knowledge of any fact implies the knowledge of the limits of that fact, in other words the knowledge of other facts. Therefore, in order to obtain results, the scientist must limit his field. He must isolate part of the universe.

Science therefore cannot be, and does not claim to be, knowledge of the Whole. Moreover, as long as it is science, and not ideology under the mask of science, it does not claim certainty; all its conclusions remain open to revision. It is not possible to have exhaustive knowledge of any fact, for every fact is linked to other facts, and no one can know them all. One can have certainty only about that which is limitless. Only knowledge of the eternal is certain knowledge; every other knowledge presupposes such knowledge. The Whole, or God, is not something that exists. It is existence itself.

Among the facts, or things, that make up the universe, there is none that causes itself. That means, there exist no thing which is brought into existence by its own nature or essence, without help from the outside. Every fact exists because of other facts. There is no flower without a plant, no plant without its medium, earth, light or air, and also these are not independent. All are parts of the Whole. Even the word 'parts' gives a wrong impression. The whole of existence, which also means the cause of all that exists, is not a collection of parts.

If by Nature we mean the sum of all phenomena, we would be wrong in saying that for Spinoza knowledge of Nature equals knowledge of God. Human knowledge of phenomena is imperfect by its very nature. The whole of such knowledge would not be knowledge of the Truth.

God, in the language of Spinoza, is unlimited being, including and causing all that exists. Since there can be no cause for God's existence, God is 'his own cause' (lat. *causa sui*). Because of his use of the word God Spinoza has been attacked from two sides. According to atheists, and to those who read atheism into his doctrine, he hypocritically used God instead of Nature in a vain attempt to appease the authorities. According to the orthodox his God has no right to be called God, not being the God of Hebrew-Christian theology.

Spinoza, whose truthfulness is evident in all his words and actions, in his letters rejected with indignation the accusation of atheism. Even if this was not enough to remove all doubt, there would remain the fact that one would have to tear the fifth book out of his 'Ethics', if one would deny that love of God is the aim of his philosophy and the culmination of wisdom.

On the other hand, Spinoza makes it obvious that his God is not a ruler or a judge, that He is not 'good' or 'jealous', that He does not exist outside the universe, or act arbitrarily, or intervene in the world. Moreover there is the point which perhaps caused his conflict with the Synagogue: his God is not a bodiless spirit. The universe is His body.

Our generation find it hard to understand the offence caused by these ideas. Only thanks to the fact that Spinoza was born in what was then the most tolerant country he died in his bed. Seventy seven years before his death Giordano Bruno was burnt by the Inquisition in Rome for similar ideas. Even in Holland tolerance had its limits. A friend of Spinoza, Adriaan Koerbagh, died in jail for writing a book in Dutch which proclaimed ideas of Spinoza.

By denying Spinoza the right to use the word God one asserts that only in the Hebrew-Christian-Islamic tradition one can speak about God. This means a rejection of all civilizations before and outside this tradition, not only those of the East, but also the pre-Christian civilizations of Europe, especially the Graeco-Roman one, in which our traditions are rooted.

Spinoza, however, did not find his God outside the tradition in which he was educated. He did not find Him in the East. The supposition that he knew anything of Buddhism is totally unproved. The Hebrew and Christian theology, which he studied, led him to his conception of God. But he purified this conception and removed its unworthy elements. These are anthropomorphism (giving God man-like characteristics), and the idea of God as a judge and king. These are the elements which give the Hebrew-Christian-Islamic tradition its power, but also intolerance, sometimes fanaticism, inclination to violence and the claim to belong to a privileged elite.

God, according to Spinoza, is existence and the source of all that exists. He creates (not: created) the universe and sustains it. Being perfect and without limits He is the reality that includes all that is real. Therefore in God and because of God everything exists, including that which we call evil. Since God does not lack anything, He cannot desire. Imagining that He created the world and mankind in order to receive praise would suppose Him imperfect. He does not create out of nothing; the universe is the activity of God according to His creative power. I might add that the use of the pronoun He is a mere convenience of language. God does not belong to any category, and so is neither personal nor impersonal, neither male nor female.

Nothing can exist outside God; if anything could, God would have limits. God is Nature, if by Nature we understand the totality of all that is. Spinoza uses 'nature' as a verb, as others had done before him. God as the cause of existence is 'naturing nature' (*natura naturans*); the total of all phenomena, being manifestation of the creating power of God, is 'natured nature' (*natura naturata*).

Spinoza has been represented as an atheist by those that wished to condemn him, and also by others that wished to annex him. Both parties have overlooked the fact that few philosophers have written more than he did to show that it is absurd to deny the existence of God. Those that deny God, according to him, must, if they are consistent, deny the possibility of any certain knowledge. In order to know the truth, one needs a basic truth, by which to distinguish truth and falsehood, just as by light one knows both light and darkness. Atheism logically leads to absolute scepticism. A consistent sceptic has nothing to say; he must remain dumb (lat. *obmutescere*).

CHAPTER 3. AGAINST ABSTRACTIONS

For twenty-four centuries people have imagined that words, especially nouns, stand for 'ideas'. To give an example: what have a collie, a labrador and a pekinese in common, to be called 'dog'? According to Plato and the 'idealists' who followed him, there exists the idea 'dog', of which all dogs are only phenomena. In the same way, just as there is some 'dog-quality' which is the essence of all dogs, they looked for some 'humanity' common to all men.

A comparison between languages is bound to cast doubt on this conception. For instance, does the idea 'bone' include fish bones? In English and in Esperanto it does, but Dutch has a separate word for fish bone. And what about 'tail'? Many animals are said to have 'tails', at least in some languages, but Icelandic has separate words for horse's tail, cow's tail, etc. Some languages know oaks, willows, etc., but no 'trees'.

Spinoza did not fall into this linguistic trap. He avoided abstractions. Words like 'dog' do not represent any idea, they are merely a help to human imagination. An 'idea', for Spinoza, is not a picture in the mind, with a problematic relation to sense data. Idea means thought, and thoughts are not passive pictures in the mind, but actions.

We would misunderstand Spinoza's thought, if we looked upon his 'God' or 'Nature' as the sum of all possible experience, in other words as an abstraction. If this is naturalism, Spinoza is not a naturalist. In order to understand what Spinoza means by 'God', we have to consider another old philosophical concept, that of substance. Let us start with an example.

A wall can be white, high, built of stone, etc. 'White', etc. are called attributes, because they do not exist by themselves. There has to be *something* which is white. 'Wall' has these attributes; it could also have others. So wall is called substance. The attributes may change. The wall might be repainted, but substance remains.

Of course the wall, too, does not exist by itself. It has to stand on something, and that something is part of something else. So one might say with Descartes that all matter is one substance. But what about mind? According to Descartes, there are at least two substances, God and matter. God created not only matter, but also every human mind, because according to him mind is independent of matter. So in fact Descartes' system postulates the existence of an incalculable number of substances. Since they exist together, there must be some relation between them. Descartes can only explain this by assuming a continuous miracle, the activity of God.

Descartes, who is rightly called the father of modern philosophy, left as his heritage a dualism which has undermined the rationality of Western thought. It reappears in the two universes of Kant, in Hegel's dialectics and in the resigned acceptance of irrationality which is common among contemporary philosophers. Spinoza dug deeper and found unity. For this reason he has been overlooked. People of the West have generally preferred the excitement of conflict to the tranquility of wisdom. Western thought suffers from a hidden duality, which renders us incapable of any real dialogue. This is the crack in the foundations of our civilization. In a sense the West has made a pact with the devil whom it created. But in the end Mephistopheles appears and Faust has to pay the price.

Now let us turn to Spinoza. He knows only one substance and he calls it God. Substance, since it is limitless, has an endless number of attributes, but man knows only two of them. They are thought and extension. They are not parts, but aspects, of the one substance. God expresses his power twofold: in thought and in extension. These words must not be translated simply by 'mind' and 'matter'. God acts in the one attribute by thinking, in the other by 'movement and rest', which is Spinoza's term for what we would call energy.

Therefore there is no room in Spinoza's system for Descartes' contrast between active mind and passive matter, or Kant's contrast between the knowable world of phenomena and the unknowable 'real' world. But of even more practical importance is the fact that Spinoza's God is not internally divided like the 'spirit' in Hegel's so-called monism, which proceeds by thesis, antithesis and synthesis to some 'higher' aim.

The effect of traditional theology in the past, and of modern political theory (which is largely, even when professedly atheist, theology under a new mask), has been the justification of dualism: man against nature, orthodoxy against heresy, progress against reaction. It is easy to forget, at least as long as one considers one's own group as destined to final success and therefore right, that dualism of any kind is fundamentally irrational. So are the hatred, oppression and destructiveness which are its practical results.

By proclaiming the unity of all that exists Spinoza gave our civilization a remedy against intolerance. Anyone who claims to know the will of God or the aim of history is bound to be intolerant. In his view tolerance would be betrayal. Spinoza understood that God has no aim, and that therefore history has no aim. The eternally existing All lacks nothing. Saying of any- that it happened according to the will of God or the laws of history, is only another way of saying that it happened.

In one of his letters Spinoza presents us with a parable. He asks us to imagine a tiny creature living in the blood. How could it know that the different ingredients of the blood together form the blood, and that blood does not exist without a body? This may help us to see the universe as one living being. All its parts exist and act according to the laws of the whole; no part could act arbitrarily.

God, or Nature, has no aim. This does not mean that teleology, purposeful activity, is lacking in Spinoza's system. Perhaps ecology, which studies the relations between living creatures, can help us here. All living beings in a certain ecological system, say a Scottish loch, exist together, each of them using the activity of others. The activity of all has the effect of maintaining or restoring harmony between its parts. Constantly individuals are being replaced, but the whole remains. The universe is maintained by the activity of its parts, which is God's activity. The aim of this striving is inter-harmony, and at the same time diversity.

According to Hegelian critics Spinoza's God is without diversity, and his Whole means Nothingness. The example of ecology helps us to refute this. For Spinoza the greatest reality or perfection means the greatest diversity.

All that exists, according to Spinoza, is either attribute or mode. The Latin of the Ethics explains *modo* as *substantiae affectio*. This is difficult to translate, in any language. Maybe modification of substance, or manner of existence, would come nearest.

The totality of phenomena is called 'the face (or form) of the whole universe' (*facies totius universi*). This is also a mode, but an infinite mode. Its origin is another infinite mode 'movement and rest' or energy. Spinoza calls these infinite modes 'eternal truths'. Apart from these, modes are facts or things caused by other facts or things. Mode is everything that is a fact in the universe: you and I, the paper on which I write, the thoughts which I write, electrons, elephants and the form of the whole universe.

Some commentators, looking through the spectacles of nineteenth century idealism, have seen in Spinoza's modes mere illusions, products of our imperfect understanding of the sole reality. This view disregards what Spinoza teaches about *conatus*, the fact that every part of the universe tries to maintain itself. Moreover, some have already pointed out that if this criticism is valid, it could also be directed against modern science. Physics reduces everything to energy. No doubt a comparison between the doctrine of Spinoza and modern science would be interesting. I have to leave this to others better qualified.

Spinoza himself took a lively interest in the science of his time, as appears in his correspondence with Oldenburg. It must not be forgotten, however, that he did not seek the support of science for his philosophy. If he could have guessed that modern science would support some of his ideas, it would hardly have impressed him. He did not feel the need of such confirmation. His 'eternal truths' are not found by induction. Generalisations, and all abstractions, are to him only helps to human imagination. Truth is found by other means.

CHAPTER 4. KNOWLEDGE AND OPINION

All awareness starts from selfawareness. This means that everyone of us, before experiencing anything, experiences oneself, that is one's body. I become aware of self when I discover that my body has limits, that there is something outside me. 'I' is born when we meet what is not-I. When I walk against a wall in the dark I know: 'Here I am, for here is something that is not I'. This knowledge is basic, not subject to error. Afterwards, using my senses, I conclude that I hit a wall. This conclusion may be mistaken; perhaps I ran into a cow. Conclusions derived from a selection inter sense data are not infallible.

It seems to me that Spinoza, speaking of 'the idea of the body', means this basic awareness. In his own terms, it is the idea of which the body is the *ideatum*. It is consciousness of the body, not thought about the body.

What matters to Spinoza is that man thinks. We are capable of thinking about our basic experiences. We have 'ideas of ideas' (*ideae idearum*). Man can know that he knows, and what he knows. Man is conscious of self, and therefore capable of selfcriticism.

By sense experience we mean consciousness of the effect of outside facts on the human body. These facts are not known as clear and distinct facts. Man is always conscious of many facts at the same time. We can be conscious only of a limited number of facts, and this is the cause of error. If we could be conscious of the whole universe at each moment, we would not err. But we are not God; our body has limits. Our conclusions about the world outside us are confused and erroneous, because they are based on unplanned 'wandering experience' (*vaga experiencia*). This kind of experience gives the first and lowest form of knowledge, which is mere opinion and capable of error.

Spinoza calls this first kind of knowledge 'imagination'. This is not the same as fantasy, though it includes it. He has nothing against imagination; it is the necessary basis of all knowledge. Rectification of understanding presupposes that there is something to understand. On condition that one treats this kind of knowledge as imagination and is aware of its imperfection, it is good (see Eth. II prop. XVII). Imagination leads astray only when it is claimed to be objective truth, for instance if fantasy becomes ideology.

Some have found a contrast between the 'rationalist' philosophy of Spinoza, according to whom imagination is confused and capable of errors, and that of the romantics, who put imagination on the throne at the expense of reason. However, Spinoza never treats imagination as something to be avoided or despised. Water matters more than the bucket, but this does not mean that one can draw water from the well without a bucket. Spinoza did not foresee, as Hegel did, the end of art because of the victory of reason. Only misunderstanding could turn Spinoza into a rationalist opposed to imagination and therefore to art. According to him imagination, which in his system includes not only art but also science, is a means, not an end. The first kind of knowledge, and also the second which is that of reason, prepare for the third and highest knowledge, intuition, in which man finds lasting happiness. It is a remarkable fact that Spinoza inspired many poets. Perhaps some of them, and especially Goethe, understood him better than did his nineteenth century commentators.

It should be stressed that it is not the artist only who does not offer, and does not claim to offer, truth which cannot be doubted. The scientist is in the same position. He remains a scientist as long as he is willing to review all his conclusions and to test his knowledge by new experiments. Any ideology that claims scientific certainty, by this very claim proves itself unscientific.

An 'idea' is any kind of consciousness about a fact. The ideas of imagination are fragmentary, confused and therefore open to error. Spinoza calls them inadequate ideas. The rectification of the understanding, which Spinoza intended to clarify in the book of that title (which remained unfinished) means rational criticism of one's ideas. Errors do not spring from wrong decisions; they are caused by lack of knowledge as a result of confused imagination. They are removed by the use of reason. It is significant, and somewhat amusing, that even those philosophers who proclaim the inadequacy of reason have to plead their cause by arguments that claim to be rational. Of course, any argumentation deliberately irrational would be mere slogan shouting, about as intelligent as Nietzsche's ravings about whips and women.

No one can doubt the fact that he doubts. On this certainty Descartes founded his philosophy. According to Spinoza doubt, which means awareness of the imperfection of our knowledge, already pre-supposes that we have the idea of a perfect being whose knowledge surpasses ours. Since we have the idea of such perfection, we can judge by it all other ideas and so rectify our understanding (TRU, VII, 38). We correct the confusion of our ideas by comparing them with objective facts.

For instance, as a result of some unpleasantness caused to us by a member of some group, nation or race, confused imagination makes us suspect or hate people of the same kind. Moreover, imagination produces abstractions which have no real existence, like race, class, etc., so we are inclined to treat people as representatives of this abstraction rather than as themselves. This confusion and prejudice can be overcome by a rational distinction between what is real and what is abstract and imaginary.

As will be explained in the next chapter, the power of God in each being shows itself as the *conatus*, the impetus or energy, of this being, by which it remains in existence and seeks to increase its power of action. In man, this 'impetus' means striving towards more reality, which can also be called striving after perfection. Confused knowledge, which means misunderstanding of the world in which we live, enslaves a man and diminishes his power of action. The way towards liberation, which is also the way to happiness, is therefore the way of rectification of the understanding. All other ways are illusive and lead to other kinds of slavery under new masters. Illustrations of this fact abound in history, especially in that of the last two centuries.

Of the two lower kinds of knowledge the first, that of imagination, is necessary but inadequate. The second, that of reason, corrects the first. Among sciences only mathematics belongs to the second kind, since it does not depend on the senses. Adequate knowledge of concrete facts comes with the third kind of knowledge, that of intuition. This knowledge becomes possible, when reason has made us aware of the necessity of each fact in the universe. 'Chance' is an illusion which belongs to the first kind of knowledge. Who understands the interconnection of all facts, knows that everything happens according to necessity. This knowledge fills the mind with joy and removes fear.

In one of his letters Spinoza wrote that it is not his custom to argue against opponents. I follow him in this, and keep silent about those who claim to give an account of Spinoza's doctrine, but leave out, or pass lightly over, its centre and culmination: intuitive knowledge. Spinoza as a 'rational egoist' is a caricature.

Since no fact stands by itself, complete knowledge of any fact would have to imply complete knowledge of the universe, that means knowledge of God or Substance. Such knowledge would be eternal happiness. Only God's intellect can have universal knowledge, but man, according to Spinoza, can acquire a knowledge of concrete things which is intuitive and errorless; knowledge 'by feeling and enjoying' (in the Dutch of the 'Short Treatise': *door een gevoelen en genieten*). It is to be remembered that errors do not arise from basic sense experience.

Errors come from imaginary thought. Because of imperfect knowledge our thinking links the elements of the world in an unplanned way, and treating this imaginary knowledge as certainty we put a screen between us and the real world. This screen has to be broken, if we are to find our way to direct experience of reality.

Our human impetus (*conatus*) will not rest in anything less than perfection, or reality. The way of reason, however, is a difficult one and many avoid it. The world offers many phony ways. Among them are emotional religion, political mass hysteria, drugs; they attract in spite of their irrationality, because they promise to open a door towards direct experience of reality, which is happiness. Spinoza does not offer an easy way. Only reason will help us to escape from illusions. Reason, however, is a tool, not an end. Reason proves, but does not make us experience, the interconnection of all that exists. This experience comes when, by the searchlight of our attention, we have found the eternal in any part of the All.

CHAPTER 5. PERSISTENCE

'All flesh is grass, and all the goodliness thereof is as the flower of the field' (Isaiah 40, 6). Indeed, but even the flower of the field lasts, if only a short while. How must we understand the existence of anything not permanent, anything less than the whole?

Grass, like man, tries to persist in its being. That which calls all things into being and makes them persist is according to Spinoza God's creative power. Every particle of the All not only exists, but persists, and its impetus (*conatus*) is a part, or more correctly a manifestation, of God's power.

All that exists strives not only to remain, but to increase its power of action. In the human body, this striving shows itself as activity; in the human mind it is 'will' or 'appetite'. When it is conscious of its aim we call it desire. When adequate, that means rational, ideas guide the human impetus, it is 'active'; when it is guided by inadequate ideas it is dependent on the outside world and therefore 'passive'.

Without impetus, that means without emotion, there would be no activity. Emotions are active when they spring from man's own nature, passive if they have external causes. Passive emotions are called passions. Obeying them man is slave to the world outside himself. Not to be slave to passions is to be free. Spinoza, in contrast to the Stoics, does not proclaim that reason can overcome passions. An emotion can only be overcome by a stronger emotion. In order to become free of the slavery of passions man should cease to desire that which is ephemeral and which one can have only by denying it to others. Freedom comes from active emotions, that means the desire of that which is permanent and not exclusive.

When man's impetus is thwarted and the power of action of mind and body decrease, the result is sorrow (*tristitia*). On the other hand, impetus that increases its power means joy (*laetitia*). From these basic emotions, together with desire, Spinoza derives all others. In his ignorance man pursues many ends, but the aim of man's impetus is reality or perfection. The mind loves that which increases its power, and hates the opposite. Men suffer, because they strive after that which by its very nature cannot satisfy them. Turning his back on these imaginary goals, man finds the way to wisdom and happiness. The quotations from TRU, in the first chapter, tell how Spinoza began to have his doubt about generally pursued aims, and how he found a good which cannot be illusive.

The key to interhuman relations is the fact that we love those that help us to reach our goal, and hate those that threaten us, or threaten that which we love. In the third part of the 'Ethics' Spinoza elaborates his theory of emotions in great detail and with convincing realism. His most important conclusion is that hatred creates or increases hatred. By love hatred can be overcome and changed into love. It is worth noticing, that the writings of Spinoza, in spite of the persecution and calumny which he met in his lifetime, lack all traces of bitterness against his opponents.

Though active emotions follow the order of reason, and passive ones spring from external conditions, neither of them happen by chance. In the universe there is no room for anything arbitrary. Since nothing happens without a cause, 'free will', if it means uncaused will, is an illusion. A free action, according to Spinoza, is an action determined by the agent. A man who knows the truth acts according to the intellect of God, for all true ideas are ideas of God, who is 'His own cause'. Free action, therefore, is the action of man as part of the Whole. By such action we express our essential nature and live in harmony, because the aim is common to all men.

A free man is a man whose emotions are active. Whilst a man is ruled by passive emotions, like hatred, sorrow, fear and envy, he lacks freedom. Spinoza did not despise all passive emotions. Love, compassion and selfconfidence can also be caused by external circumstances, and they can result in conduct similar to that of a free man. Such conduct, however, will remain constant and will last in spite of difficulties only if the agent is not ruled by passions.

Spinoza was well aware of the strength of passive emotions; he wrote that men are 'naturally inclined to envy and hatred'. But no less naturally, according to him, man is capable of forming adequate ideas, which lead to active emotions and thereby to harmony between people. The quality of a person who acts according to active emotions he calls *fortitudo*, perhaps best translated by 'strength of mind'. A free man acts according to the intellect of God, in whom there are no divisions. By his conduct he is bound to promote harmony between men. He lives without hatred or self-pity; he tolerates and forgives those whose conduct is the result of confused ideas. The life of Spinoza is an inspiring example of this strength of mind. The collection of his letters, according to Goethe, is 'the most interesting book in the world from the point of view of sincerity and love of men'.

Spinoza uses 'necessity' as the opposite of 'chance', not of 'freedom'. God, being his own cause, acts freely and necessarily. A free man acts not capriciously, but according to the necessity of his nature. If this is to be called determinism, it should be remembered that determinists usually hold that the future can be foretold if one knows the laws that determine it, which can be sociological, psychological or physio-chemical. Spinoza denies this possibility. Only the intellect of God would be capable of knowing all the facts and their interrelation, and the laws that determine future facts.

By paying attention to this part of the doctrine of Spinoza our generation might be able to overcome the different theories inherited from the nineteenth century, which still rule the world and divide mankind. Spinoza shows the confusion out of which they were born.

CHAPTER 6. QUALITY

According to the Hebrew-Christian-Islamic or monotheist tradition God created the universe out of nothing and exists outside it. God rules the world, pursuing some aim, and intervenes in it according to His will. Men, being in the world, are outside God; our knowledge of Him depends on revelation. God at certain points of time came into the world, 'took flesh' or spoke to men through prophets. Knowledge about God therefore is possible only to those to whom He revealed Himself, and to the others that believe them, or at least believe those among them who appear the most credible, because the revealers do not always agree. In most cases people accept the beliefs of the community to which they belong, or those that give them an emotional satisfaction which seems to justify these beliefs.

If our knowledge about life's purpose depends on revelation, ethics must also depend on revelation, which in practice means on those who put into words the revelation which we accept. In that case the will of God has to be proclaimed by a sacred community or a sacred book. Such at least is the theory. History shows that in practice people may accept some ethical doctrine even though they contradict the revelation which they claim to believe. For instance, in spite of the fact that Jesus in the New Testament preaches love to enemies and forbids oaths, Christians for centuries have killed and sworn without any bad conscience.

In contrast to all this Spinoza based his ethics on reason. It is an ethical system not for believers, but for all men. It does not demand obedience, but understanding.

According to Spinoza, the word 'good' cannot be meaningfully used for God or Nature, or for any part of Nature. The universe does not exist to serve men, and therefore can be neither good nor bad. Good is that which is useful to men. Whilst men have no knowledge higher than imagination, their ideas about good and bad are bound to disagree, for they do not have the same needs. Spinoza illustrates this by an example: 'Music is good for the melancholy, bad for mourners, and indifferent for the deaf.'

This does not mean, however, that 'good' can only be used subjectively. Man, once he has understood that desires based on confused imagination do not show the way to happiness, will seek that which is good under all circumstances. The true good for men is that which furthers man's striving after reality, or perfection. Good is that which helps me and others to attain perfect humanity, the happiness which is the result of intuitive knowledge. This is not an illusory aim belonging to some Utopia, though it is not within easy reach. Spinoza formulates it as 'the knowledge of the unity of the mind with all Nature' (TRU II, 13).

Spinoza based his ethic on his understanding of man's nature. Some philosophers deny the possibility of such a base. According to them, that which is to be done, the subject of ethics, has no connection with what in fact exists; there can be no derivation of 'ought' from 'is'. They are bound to deny this, when they do not accept that man's striving (*conatus*) is part of the All, that means of God in his creative power. This denial leads to an ethic which exalts 'duty'; man is said to act morally only when he acts against his natural inclination. Spinoza rejects the idea of a 'will' opposed to God. Not evil will, but confused knowledge is the source of bad conduct, that means of conduct which diminishes man's power to act and makes man passive.

Though Spinoza derives 'good' and 'bad' from an understanding of man, and does not call God or Nature in as a lawgiver, he is no relativist in relation to morals. The different kinds of relativism, which we inherited from past generations, claim that good or bad have no objective significance, but depend on changing conditions which can be clarified by either sociology or psychology. Such relativisms are inconsistent, and therefore self-destructive. They proclaim a fact about morals, which according to their own theory they have no right to do. To give an example, those that proclaim that morals depend on economics, if they are right, say nothing about morals, only something about the real or imagined economic interests of the intellectuals who invented the theory. Therefore an honest relativist can only keep silent (*obmutescere*) like Spinoza's sceptic.

Some of Spinoza's critics, already among his contemporaries, have asked how according to Spinoza anything can be bad, if all actions are God's actions. Does a criminal do God's will in the same way as a well behaved person? Spinoza replied that bad intentions, hatred and violence are negative; they spring from confused knowledge, not from God. Spinoza was not the first thinker who derived bad actions from lack of knowledge. Socrates held the same opinion. Aristotle disagreed with him, and to many the words of the apostle Paul come to mind (Rom. 7, 19): 'The good that I would I do not, but the evil which I would not, that I do'. Spinoza was well aware of this; in Eth. IV he quotes a similar saying from Ovid's Metamorphoses. Perhaps he would have replied, and present ideas about the subconscious would support him, that unfree people, which means the majority, are of two minds. Few people know what they want.

All doctrines that treat 'sin' as revolt against God, limit the power of God, introduce some power over which God has no control and break the unity of the universe. Spinoza's doctrine honours God. The All, which we can call God, Nature or Substance, lacks nothing and is perfect in every detail. Reason does not see in the universe a collection of indistinguishable items. Perfection consists of the greatest possible variety. An amoeba, a whale and a man all exist because of their 'impetus', but they are not similar. Their degree of 'reality' depends on their capacity for autonomous action. One of the key phrases, which opens the very heart of Spinoza's system, is found in the last chapter of Eth. I: 'God did not lack material for creating all things from the highest to the lowest'. Eminent people are those who strive after an aim that is eternal and common to all men. In seeking their own good they seek the good of all.

Man's quality is determined by the object of his love. Love for impermanent objects causes fear, envy and finally disappointment. Hatred is even more destructive than irrational love. A free man does not hate. It is irrational even to hate that which is bad. If there were really such a thing as a devil, he would be an object for pity, not hatred (ST). A wise man's attitude towards the troubles of life is what is called stoical, though not based on a stoic contempt for emotions.

In our days, at least in the rich parts of the world, men have accustomed themselves to consider disappointments and hardships as something that should not be, something against which one seeks help from a pill or a visit to a psychiatrist. Many people have lost the resilience of more realistic generations, of which speaks the Dutch poet Vondel, Spinoza's contemporary, in a well known strophe:

> Blessed a mind that will not yield,
> that not in ease its strength forgoes,
> holding out firmly like a shield
> against inevitable blows.

Spontaneity in a free man is rational; he needs neither fear nor hope to activate him. He finds nothing in the world that would be worthy of contempt, hatred or ridicule. Spinoza warns that pity, if it is not based on reason, can lead to foolish actions, but that a man not moved by compassion, whether rational or passional, would be inhuman.

Spinoza, who himself lived very simply, did not approve of asceticism. According to the 'Ethics' joy is always good; one can never have too much of it. A free man lives virtuously, but not because he fears divine punishment or human disapproval. There is no reason why the wise should not find refreshment in 'sweet odour of flowers, beauty of green plants, ornaments, music, arts and theatre and all that can give refreshment without doing harm'. (Eth. IV, 45).

Knowing that nothing that seems frightening is really to be feared, a free man is courageous but not imprudent. He is helpful and unselfish, for the good which he seeks is the good of all. Lies and betrayals are to be avoided, even if they might save one's life, for social life cannot exist without trust among men. Like Kant, Spinoza held that man has no right to treat himself as an exception.

CHAPTER 7. POLITICS

If man's existence has a beginning but no end, if our short earthly life is only a preparation for eternal bliss or torment and if only the church can save from torment, political theory should depend on theology. A good state would be the kind of state that serves the good of man as it is proclaimed by the church. An independent study of politics only came into its own after the end of the Middle Ages, when Machiavelli and Hobbes considered the state as an artifice or even a work of art. But even a work of art must serve some end. According to Machiavelli the end of the state is power, but power to do what? Spinoza's criticism of him is that he gives no aim to his state. According to Hobbes the state is needed because men are by nature hostile to one another and therefore need some authority which they obey because of fear. To Spinoza, however, people ruled by fear are hardly human.

Spinoza's political theory, found in TTP which appeared in 1670 and in TP which was published unfinished after his death is hardly understandable without the base found in his 'Ethics'. In this, his main work, Spinoza shows that the only way towards freedom is the way of reason, which leads to intuitive knowledge not open to doubt. If all men lived according to reason, there would be no need for state power. Since this is not the case, and since it would be a utopian dream to expect this in some future time, men need a state, which should make reasonable life possible by means of suitable laws and institutions. The state cannot make people rational, but it can lead to rational conduct. In other words, human institutions (or culture, though Spinoza and his contemporaries did not use this word) should be a school for reasonableness. No man can be forced to be rational, therefore institutions must leave freedom to opinions. The real enemies of peace and order are not the doubters, but those that try to suppress other people's opinions.

Theologians speak of the will of God, which men can obey or disobey. In other words, they proclaim a God who is doing his best to govern the universe, but not in fact governs. For Spinoza the 'will of God' is meaningless. Nothing could happen unless

God caused it. He acts in a virtuous man and also in a tyrant or robber. The universe is one; never and nowhere it is without God. The laws of God are the laws of nature; no one could disobey them. God is no lawgiver; divine law cannot be the base of human society.

From Hobbes Spinoza borrowed the idea of a 'contract'. Men once came to an agreement, so that every one yielded his 'right', which means nothing but power, to some ruler. This idea of a 'social contract' has a long history. A century after Spinoza it became an important element in the political philosophy of Rousseau, which influenced the French revolution. Spinoza probably regarded it not as a fact of history, rather as a theoretical clarification. He does not mention it in his last work. The importance of the contract theory lies in the fact that it derives ruling authority not from God or Nature, but from men.

Rulers exist to regulate the conduct of the citizens in order to make living together possible. They should not, however, try to regulate the thinking of the ruled; this will only lead to hypocrisy. The state should tolerate all kinds of religious ideas. In order that freedom of opinion may be maintained the church should not be a state within the state; it should not try to rule the rulers.

No doubt Spinoza, in this, supported the interests of the class to which Holland owed its religious freedom (which was far from being absolute). The 'regents', as they were called, were rich merchants who favoured tolerance. The Calvinist church had no use for tolerance and wanted to have the last word in political matters. Once the two parties had fought side by side against the Catholic absolutism of the King of Spain. When the Netherlands became independent, even while the eighty-years struggle was still going on, their interests clashed. The 'regents' paid the salaries of the ministers of the state church, but, in spite of this, the church had a strong position and did not always obey. The poor depended on the church as the distributor of alms; for instance in Amsterdam alone half a million guilders a year was spent on charity. The poorer classes generally could be counted upon to support the church against the rulers. They also supported the Prince of Orange, the head of the army, whose political interests coincided with those of the church. This situation explains why Spinoza suggested that the state, not the church, should look after the poor.

It cannot be said, however, that Spinoza in the class conflict of his day supported the 'haves' against the 'have-nots'. The Calvinist church gave its blessing to striving after wealth; Spinoza considered such striving foolish and an obstacle to happiness. He was never rich, nor did he try to become rich, and no doubt he was well acquainted with the darker aspect of Holland's 'golden age' – the many unemployed or poorly paid workers. He probably considered oligarchy preferable to monarchy, at least for the Netherlands. Democracy did not exist in his time. He knew it only through classical authors and apparently favoured it. His main interest, however, was not who should rule, but how one should rule.

Spinoza was a strong defender of the 'open', non-ideological society. This, more than anything else, makes his political ideas important after three centuries. Today the enemies of the open society are political rather than religious ideologists. Instead of the superstitious belief in the 'pie in the sky', which gave power to the churches, now freedom is threatened by a belief no less superstitious in spite of its claim to scientific truth, the belief in inevitable progress, the secrets of which the ideologists claim to understand. The door towards liberty, which Spinoza opened, Hegel tried to shut again, not without success. Hegel proclaimed a new god, history, manifesting itself in dialectic progress. The choice of the phases of this progress can only be subjective. The theory gives power to ideologists, who may be idealist or materialist, right or left.

Any certainty based on history would be to Spinoza nothing but idolised imagination. By his historical study of the Bible he intended to destroy the illusion that reports of past happenings (which are bound to be fragmentary and subjective) can give knowledge about the unchanging All. Hegel, who identified God and history, is the most consistent and the most successful opponent of all that Spinoza stood for.

Perhaps today, after three hundred years, some of us are again inclined to listen to Spinoza's quiet voice between the noise of slogans, bombs and rockets. Hegel and the industrial revolution have had their triumphs. Men have trampled on Nature; they have oppressed and exterminated one another in the sacred name of Progress. Whilst true scientists know that science does not give final truth, politicians have claimed scientific certainty for their ideologies. By means of the irrational romantic doctrine of Hegel the 'closed society' has counter-attacked in order to destroy the budding tolerance. The 'irresistible march of Progress', like the 'irresistible grace' of the theologians, cannot tolerate independent thought. It has to be said, moreover, that freedom without the discipline of thinking is not likely to survive and does not deserve to. The defenders of liberty too often lack the rational and religious base, the rock on which Spinoza founded his philosophy. The 'empiricist' philosophy, which is the ruling one in the English-speaking countries, is a weak base. Only too often relativists and sceptics end up by licking the boots of the men of violence, on the left or the right.

Spinoza took from the state its theological base, its authority 'by the grace of God', but he did not leave it as a mere instrument for maintaining the status quo. He criticized Hobbes, who wanted an absolute ruler and citizens ruled by fear. Spinoza considered fear one of the passions which one should avoid whenever possible. A free people obeys because of hope, not fear. 'The aim of the state is not to change rational beings into animals or automata, but on the contrary to make it possible for them to use their mental and physical powers, and to prevent them from fighting one another because of hatred, anger, distrust and malice. The aim of the state is freedom.' Sovereignty should exist with the approval of the people, otherwise it would be based on conquest and the citizens would be slaves obeying only because of fear.

Since rights have no meaning without power to enforce them, Spinoza is a realist about interstate relations. Treaties are honoured as long as they serve the interest of both parties. One might add to this that in our days states will live in peace only if they fear war more than they fear one another.

Any government that acts against that which the majority of its citizens considers its interest, acts foolishly and endangers its power. Despotism results in rebellion; if this happens it is the rulers, not the citizens, who are to blame. On the other hand, a virtuous body of citizens is due to good government.

In the introduction to TPP Spinoza praised his native country: 'We have the rare happiness of living in a republic where everyone's opinion is free, when people can worship God according to their conscience and where liberty is esteemed above anything else'. But no more than two years after the appearance of the book the party that favoured tolerance was temporarily eclipsed and their leader John de Witt murdered. Long before this, the process against Koerbagh had shown that it was dangerous to proclaim Spinoza's ideas, even in Holland and in his native city Amsterdam, which he had called in his book 'that remarkable city, where men of different sects and nations live together in peace'. His ideas, if understood, remain dangerous wherever freedom is feared.

The main weapon of those ideologists who consider themselves the instruments of divine or historical necessity is moral indignation, in spite of their relativism about morals. One persecutes with conviction only if one considers the opponent not only wrong but also evil. An antidote against this venom is the rationality of Spinoza. He sees man as a natural phenomenon, not to be worshipped or condemned, but to be understood.

To rational people an earthly paradise waiting for us after 'the' revolution is as incredible as a paradise after death. The jackbooted 'march of history', evoked in political speeches, seems to lead not towards progress in any real sense, but to hatred among men, pollution and waste of resources. Some of us have begun to look at Nature without nineteenth century spectacles. We see in the non-human world more collaboration than destructiveness, a community to form part of rather than materials to be used. A new attitude is coming into being, which may well be the original attitude of mankind: man not as enemy and conqueror, but as part of Nature. In the human world, instead of masses fit only to be manure on the fields of the future, we see people, different but capable of understanding one another. And we remember what Spinoza said about the greatest good: 'the knowledge of the unity of the mind with all Nature' (TRU II, 13).

CHAPTER 8. THE LIFE OF SPINOZA

On Thursday 27th July 1656 the Jewish congregation of Amsterdam met in the Synagogue for a frightening ceremony. While the believers responded 'amen' to every phrase of the rabbi's loud proclamation, the lamps were put out, one after another. Finally the last burning candles were dipped in a bowl of blood, and in the darkness the ram's horns sounded shrilly. The community excommunicated one of its members – Baruch de Spinoza. He himself was not present. Otherwise he would have had to lie on the threshold, whilst all men walked over him.

Here are some of the words of the curse:

> 'According to the judgment of the angels and the decree of the saints we condemn, curse and excommunicate Baruch de Spinoza, with the consent of the eternal God and this entire holy community, according to the holy books of the Law and its 613 commandments, with the curse by which Joshua cursed Jericho, with the curse by which Elisha cursed the boys, and with all the curses found in the Law. May he be accursed by day and by night, accursed lying down and rising up, accursed going out and going in... We warn that nobody must have any dealings with him by mouth or letter, that nobody in any way show him favour, that nobody stay with him under one roof, that nobody come within four yards distance of him, that nobody read anything that he has written.'

The 'terrible heresies and black misdeeds' for which he was cursed were doubts about Hebrew theology and non-observance of the Sabbath and food regulations. Spinoza was then twenty-four years old. In 1678, a year after his death, he was again condemned, this time by the Dutch government, which forbade the sale of his 'posthumous works', which had just appeared. They included his 'Ethics'. In little more than twenty years Spinoza gave the world not only the most convincing philosophical system, but also the exemplary life of a sage, a living illustration of the precept of his 'Ethics': 'Hatred is not overcome by hatred, but by love'.

It was not surprising that the Jews of Amsterdam feared nonconformity; they themselves were a community of ex-apostates. When in 1496 the Arabs of Spain, who tolerated them, were defeated, the Jews became subject to persecution by the Catholic kings of Spain. Many of them fled to Portugal. Soon in that country, too, they had to choose between exile and acceptance of Catholicism. Many of them conformed. Christians regarded them with suspicion and called them Marrans, which is said to mean pigs. They themselves, in whispers, spoke of themselves as *anussim*, 'the forced', and kept Hebrew traditions secretly alive in their homes. When in 1580 the King of Spain conquered Portugal many of the Marrans sought refuge in Amsterdam, the most important city of the rebellious Dutch nation, which since 1568, successfully in spite of many hardships, defied the Spanish empire. There they soon returned to the religion of their fathers. The city's rulers did not confine them to any 'ghetto', but they themselves preferred to live together. The 'Jewish quarter' of Amsterdam existed till the German occupation of Holland in the second World War, when the Nazis led the inhabitants away and butchered them.

For the toleration, which they found in Holland, they did not have to thank the Calvinist state church. The republic had no strong central government. The towns were ruled by families of rich merchants who were called 'regents'. Commerce led to tolerance, and among the regents there were people with new ideas. Descartes (1596 - 1650), the father of modern philosophy, who was a French Catholic, sought and found a refuge in the Protestant Netherlands. Not only among the regents were there people critical of the state church. After his excommunication Spinoza made friends among Mennonites and Collegiants, sects whose members were largely small traders or artisans without political power. The Mennonites were, and are, a Dutch Protestant sect, which was widespread already before the arrival of Calvinism. They do not seek political power and disapprove of infant baptism, war and oaths. Under Spanish rule thousands of them died as victims of Catholic persecution. Under the republic they were tolerated; the regents did not allow the state church to harass them too much. Even more important in Spinoza's life was the Collegiant sect, a group of undogmatic Christians, who had their centre in the village of Rijnsburg.

Spinoza's biographers have no easy task, for the great philosopher never wrote anything which was meant to give information about his personal life. This was not due to a desire for secrecy. People of the seventeenth century did not see any point in showing their personality naked to the world. This fashion came a century later, with the 'Confessions' of Rousseau. Moreover, Spinoza believed that true ideas are ideas that exist in God's mind; the person who proclaims them is of little importance. He wrote his 'Ethics' in mathematical style in order to make it as impersonal as possible. Personal notes are sounded only in the first chapters of TRU, where he speaks of his doubts about the accepted values and his search for what is permanent.

Biographers have found, however, that Baruch's father was a merchant, that three times death robbed him of a wife, and that Baruch's mother was his second wife. She died as early as 1636, probably of tuberculosis, which was also to cause her son's death. At home Portuguese was spoken, but the language written was Spanish. Young Baruch, who was also called Bento, and later, latinised, Benedictus (all three names mean 'blessed'), learned Hebrew thoroughly in a boys' school under the famous rabbi Morteira. His later works show that he acquired a profound knowledge of the Old Testament and the comments of Hebrew scholars. He must have had a talent for languages. He spoke Dutch with non-Jews, and afterwards learned Latin, French, Italian and perhaps German. He never learned English.

In TTP Spinoza mentions Maimonides, or Mose ben Maimon, a Hebrew theologian, who lived under tolerant Arab rulers in Cordoba and Cairo (1135-1204). Maimonides tried to find a compromise between religion and reason. Spinoza rejected his allegorical explanation of difficult Biblical texts, and preferred to accept that the Bible can err, but his way of thinking is nearer to that of Maimonides than to Descartes' dualism, as Roth has shown. Spinoza began to learn Latin probably when he was about eighteen years old, and so opened a door to a new dimension of thought outside the Hebrew tradition.

Only after his father's death Spinoza's unorthodox views began to give offence. Perhaps out of respect he hid his doubts while his father lived. For a short time he together with his half-brother continued his father's business, not very successfully as it seems. After his excommunication he was left clanless and homeless, but his friends found for him a place to live and work as a corrector. Soon he learned to polish lenses, and by this trade he earned enough to satisfy his modest needs.

Spinoza's correspondence, which was published after his death, shows that he was a good and faithful friend. In that period, when learned periodicals did not yet exist, correspondence between scholars was of the greatest importance. Spinoza, however, did not write to scholars only. Many of his friends were people who could learn from him, but had nothing to teach him.

One of his correspondents, Pieter Balling, wrote a booklet 'The Light on the Candlestick' declaring that each man has an 'inner light', an idea also found among Quakers. This light is described in Spinozistic terms as the light of reason – Christ in every man. Perhaps Spinoza had contacts with the Quakers. In 1657 the English Quaker William Ames visited Amsterdam and met an excommunicated Jew who spoke to him about Christ. This can hardly have been anyone but Spinoza. Though he never became a Christian, he wrote in TPP, V: 'If one has no knowledge of the Bible, but has right opinions and lives according to true principles, he is blessed (*beatus*) and has in him the spirit of Christ'. In one of his letters to Oldenburg we read: 'I say that it is not essential to salvation to know Christ according to the flesh' (this must mean, according to the teachings of the church) 'but this cannot be said about the eternal Son of God, which is the eternal Wisdom of God, which shows itself in everything, especially in the human mind, but most of all in Jesus Christ.' Such ideas about Christ might be acceptable to the Quakers, as they were to his Collegiant friends.

One element in the life-style of many Christian sects of his day, which they had in common with the Calvinists, was that which is now called puritanism, somewhat unjustly, because it is much older than the puritan movement, even than Christianity. Their suspicion of amusement, laughter, joy was a result of dualism between spirit and nature. Spinoza, who had overcome this dualism in his philosophy, protested in his 'Ethics' against this fear of joy (Eth. IV, 42, 45).

There was no puritanism in the 'cheerful doctor', his new friend and teacher, Francis van der Enden, who ran a 'Latin school' in Amsterdam. Spinoza stayed with him for several years. He was a refugee from the South, the present Belgium, which was still under the Spaniards. Till he was forty he was a Jesuit, then he left the order, married and had six children, all, it was said, as intelligent as he. Van der Enden was a physician as well as a Latin scholar, and was greatly interested in the new physics. Under his guidance Spinoza studied Latin, which he had already begun to learn and became acquainted not only with the classical writers, whom he later sometimes quoted, but also with the old atomic philosophy of Democritus and Epicurus, and with the new thought of Descartes.

Spinoza did not accept the Cartesian philosophy, but mastered it well enough to explain it in mathematical form. The only book that appeared under his own name in his lifetime does not deal with his own philosophy, but with that of Descartes. This shows that for Spinoza argumentation by means of axioms and propositions, which he later used in his 'Ethics', was not a proof of truth, but a useful method of clarification.

At this time he also learned Italian, and perhaps studied the works of Giordano Bruno and Lucilio Vanini, both victims of the Inquisition, who had been burnt because of ideas not unlike those of Spinoza's. But their influence remains unproved, for regrettably nothing indicates whether he read them or not.

Between 1656 and 1661, the year in which Spinoza moved to Rijnsburg, Spinozism was born. In those years he laid the foundations of his philosophy. The 'Short Treatise' (ST), written in that time, lost, but rediscovered in the nineteenth century, already has the basic idea of the 'Ethics'. The text is Dutch, but it may well be a translation from an original Latin made by one of his friends.

In this period Spinoza also studied the new theories about politics of the Italian Machiavelli, the Englishman Hobbes and his fellow-countryman Hugo de Groot (Grotius), who founded the study of international law with his book *De jure belli ac pacis*, 'About the laws of war and peace', of 1625. The fruits of these studies were not to appear till 1670, in TTP.

Van der Enden's home was cheerful; the family amused themselves with singing and theatrics. Even the daughters were well educated. Clara Maria, the oldest, learned Latin well enough to help with the teaching. Spinoza stayed with them not only as a pupil, but also as a teacher of Hebrew. Some biographers have imagined Spinoza in love with Clara Maria, but the girl was then thirteen years old! She afterwards married Dirck Kerkrinck, another pupil, who became a doctor. He remained Spinoza's friend till the end; one of several physicians in that circle of friends. Biographers may regret it, but there is no evidence that Spinoza ever showed any interest in women.

Among his friends Spinoza was a leader; his intellectual qualities could not remain hidden. One could even speak of an early Spinozistic movement. Simple merchants belonged to it, like Jarig Jelles and Simon de Vries. The first sold his business to dedicate himself to philosophy. De Vries wanted to make Spinoza his heir, but the philosopher refused. When finally De Vries left him an annual sum of 500 guilders Spinoza accepted, but only on condition that the sum should be reduced to 300, because this was enough for him. Another was Pieter Balling, author of 'The Light on the Candlestick'; one of Spinoza's letters was written to comfort him, when he had lost a child. Among the friends was also Jan Rieuwerts, the bookseller who published his works, the physicians Meyer and Bouwmeester, and the able translator Glazemaker, who made Dutch translations not only of the works of Descartes and Montaigne, but also, courageously, of the Koran, which he translated from the French as he did not know Arabic. They were all people with wide interests, who searched for truth and did not fear to go new ways.

One of his friends became a martyr of Spinozism. Adriaan Koerbagh composed a Dutch dictionary, but used it to proclaim ideas of Spinoza in the people's language. Calvinist ministers accused him of blasphemy. The rulers of Amsterdam did not prevent his condemnation. He died in jail.

In 1661 Spinoza moved to Rijnsburg, a village near the university town of Leiden. He had two rooms in the house of Herman Homan, a Collegiant. One was his study and bedroom, in the other he polished lenses. Visitors can see his writing desk and his work bench. He wanted to write and looked for quiet, but there was no lack of visitors. His Amsterdam friends were no doubt welcome, when they came by horsedrawn canal barge, the usual means of transport. But there were also curious students from Leiden, who perhaps interrupted his writing or polishing.

He wrote many letters, in Latin and Dutch. He began his main work, the 'Ethics', and sent parts of it to Amsterdam, where his friends discussed them. A lively interest in the new natural sciences appears in his letters to Oldenburg, a German who had moved to England and had become secretary of the newly formed Royal Society of Science. Spinoza corresponded with him about the experiments of Boyle, whose English works he could not read; he himself made some experiments with saltpetre to judge Boyle's conclusions.

After two years he left Rijnsburg and moved to Voorburg, near The Hague, perhaps in order to find more peace and quiet, or to be nearer to his protectors, the government of the 'regents' and their leader John de Witt.

It is not certain whether he ever met de Witt personally, but some leading men in De Witt's party supported him. In these days Spinoza interrupted the writing of his 'Ethics' and wrote a book on politics, TTP. No doubt De Witt's party would welcome a book that denied the church's right to rule the state. Spinoza himself in a letter to Oldenburg mentioned three reasons for writing it: the need to counteract the prejudice of the theologians, his wish to prove that he was not an atheist, and the need to defend liberty of thought which was more and more threatened by the arrogance of the ecclesiastics. The book appeared in 1670. It was anonymous, and according to the titlepage 'published in Hamburg'. But soon it was known that Spinoza was the author and Rieuwerts in Amsterdam the publisher.

It enraged the opponents, not so much because of its political ideas, as because it cast doubt on miracles and took a critical look at the text of the Bible. Spinoza did not lose his peace of mind. He trusted the regents, who in fact protected him. But during his stay in Voorburg he began to use a seal with a rose and the Latin word *caute*, 'prudently'. Did he want to proclaim his prudence, or warn the world that a rose has thorns (Spanish *espinosas*)? Perhaps both, but there is no doubt that he became more careful. On hearing that his friend Glazemaker prepared a Dutch edition of TPP he asked him not to publish it yet; it would offend even more. In fact the Dutch translation appeared only in 1693, as it said 'published in Bremen'.

In 1669 Spinoza moved to The Hague, and from 1671 he lived in the house of Hendrik van der Spijck, housepainter and portraitist; he stayed there till his death. In 1672 John de Witt's policy failed. Louis XIV, the French sun-king, whom he trusted as an ally, turned against Holland and formed an alliance with Charles II of England, who had been glad to accept Dutch hospitality during his exile in the days of Cromwell, and two aggressive German bishops. Soon a large part of the country was occupied. The province Holland was saved because water stopped the enemy, but the people panicked. The Orangists and Calvinists accused John de Witt of treason. Among the pamphlets that attacked him, one mentioned that among his books there was TPP, 'a book forged in Hell by an apostate Jew with the Devil's own help, which was published with the knowledge of De Witt and his accomplices'.

In August 1672 John de Witt and his brother Cornelius were lynched by a crowd. It happened in a square in the middle of The Hague, where now their statue stands. Their mutilated bodies were hung on the gallows. None of the murderers was punished. Some ministers spoke of God's judgment.

Spinoza's stoical self-control, which excommunication and abuse could not disturb, broke down on that occasion. He wanted to leave the house and nail a proclamation with the words *ultimi barbarorum*, 'extreme barbarians', on the door of the church where the minister had preached against De Witt. His host Van der Spijck prevented him by locking the door, and so probably saved his life. In De Witt the bigoted crows tore the greatness of the freest republic of Europe to pieces. The flowering of free thought was passed for the time being. The 'closed society' triumphed. We of the twentieth century know only too well what this means.

In the meanwhile the French army occupied a great part of the Netherlands including the town of Utrecht in the centre. Spinoza was invited to go there and meet the French marshal Condé, who had some unconventional ideas about religion. He had heard about Spinoza and wanted to meet him. Spinoza travelled through the two armies with special permit, and with the knowledge of the Dutch authorities, who perhaps hoped that the meeting might lead to peace negotiations. However, nothing came of it; Condé had already been recalled to France. Spinoza stayed in Utrecht for a few weeks, disputed with some scholars, both French and Dutch, and went home. After his return some people demonstrated against him in front of the house. Spinoza told his host that he was ready to talk to them. 'I went to Utrecht with the consent of the authorities; I am a good republican,' he said. He seems to have satisfied the demonstrators.

In 1673 Spinoza was invited to become a professor of philosophy at the university of Heidelberg. He refused politely, in the first place because he wanted to study rather than teach, and secondly because he doubted whether such a position would leave him freedom of opinion. In the Netherlands, however, reaction was riding high and the tide ran against Spinoza. TTP was forbidden in 1674, perhaps at the request of the Prince of Orange himself. William III, the later King of Great Britain and Ireland, could hardly have liked its anti-monarchical tone. The prince, however, had his merits as a leader of war. In 1674 the republic's territory was free of enemies and the war went on in other people's lands. England saw its navy beaten by the famous admiral De Ruyter and made peace. Spain, former enemy and now rival of France, joined the republic's side, and so did Sweden.

Though circumstances did not favour Spinoza he had his friends. He did not lack visitors and correspondents. Among them were scholars of international fame, like the Germans Tschirnhaus, with whom he corresponded, and Leibniz, the only one of his contemporaries who could really understand his philosophy. Leibniz and Spinoza met in Van der Spijck's house: Spinoza, 43 years old and suffering of tuberculosis which was to cause his death the following year, and the ambitious 30-year-old Leibniz, who later tried to minimise the importance of their contact.

In spite of his illness and the growing hostility of the world Spinoza lived happily. He was on friendly footing with the Van der Spijck family. Sundays, when they came from church, he joined them to drink a glass of wine, and at their request he answered their religious problems, when the sermon had been difficult to understand. He reassured Mrs. van der Spijck, when she doubted whether her religion would lead her to salvation. He made a Dutch translation of the first five books of the Old Testament, perhaps for language practice, but the translation did not satisfy him and he burned it a few days before his death. He also wrote a Hebrew grammar in Latin.

TP was his last book, but he did not finish it. It deals with politics, like TTP, but does not mention theology, perhaps in order to avoid new trouble with theologians. It contains realistic descriptions of monarchy and aristocracy, but regrettably he died before he could write the chapter on democracy. For some months he and his friends knew that the end was near. On Sunday 21st February 1677, while the Van de Spijck family was in church, he died peacefully.

He was buried in the 'New Church' of The Hague. Six carriages with leading citizens followed his coffin. The Lutheran minister Colerus, who did not accept his philosophy but admired him as a man, wrote his biography. Facts about his life he learned from Van der Spijck and his family, who honoured his memory.

His friends in Amsterdam received his desk, in which he had locked the manuscript of his 'Ethics'. At once they began to prepare the publication of his works in Latin with a Dutch translation. Already in the same year the Latin *Opera Postuma* appeared, and in 1678 the translation. But in June of that year the government stopped the sale of his books as 'profane', atheistic and blasphemous'.

In the century that followed few people knew anything about Spinoza and some of those few, who included Voltaire and Hume, misunderstood him and rejected his ideas. In his native country he did not find honour till the nineteenth century. In The Hague his statue stands in front of the house where he lived and died. But for three hundred years few have understood the heritage which he left to mankind.